An Official Neko Atsume Book

Neko Atsume Kitty Collector Haiku

SEASONS OF THE KITTY

D1280151

Original Concept by Hit-Point

TABLE OF CONTENTS

NEKO ATSUME: KITTY COLLECTOR HAIKU—SEASONS OF THE KITTY

SPRING

SUMMER

AUTUMN

WINTER

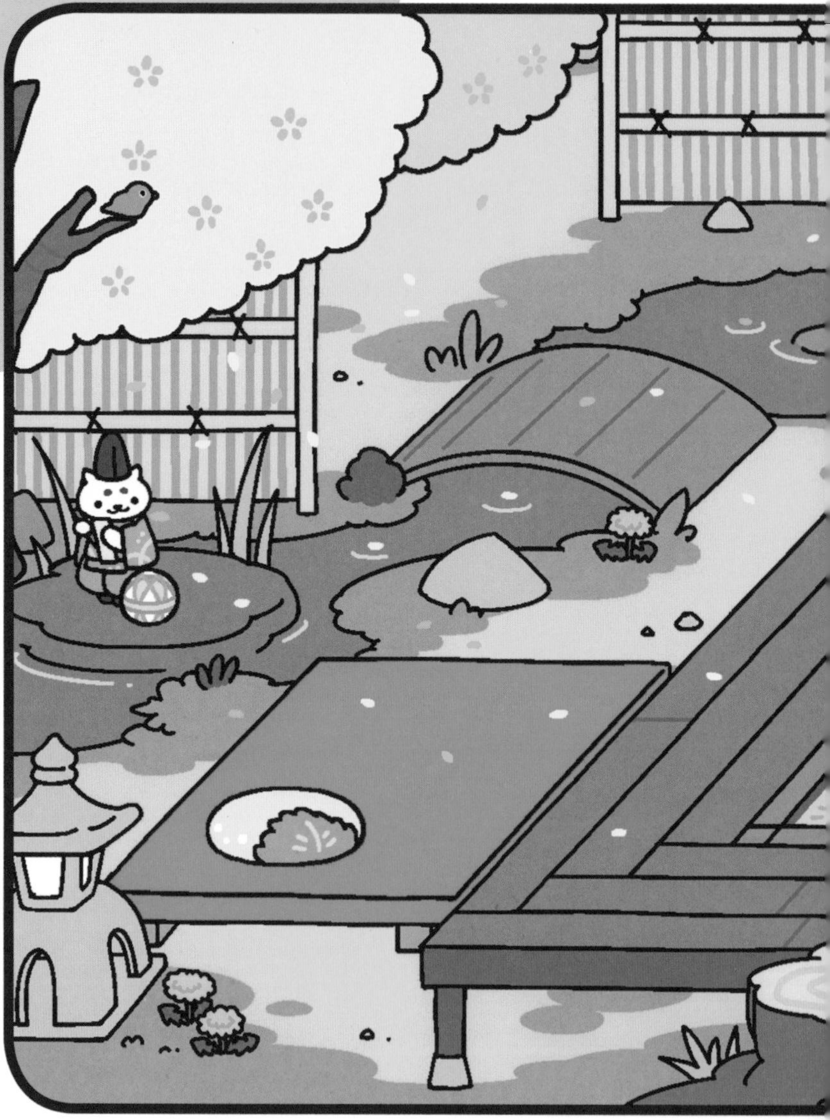

SPRING

Fortune in the house,
Bringing good luck to everyone—
Beckoning kitty.

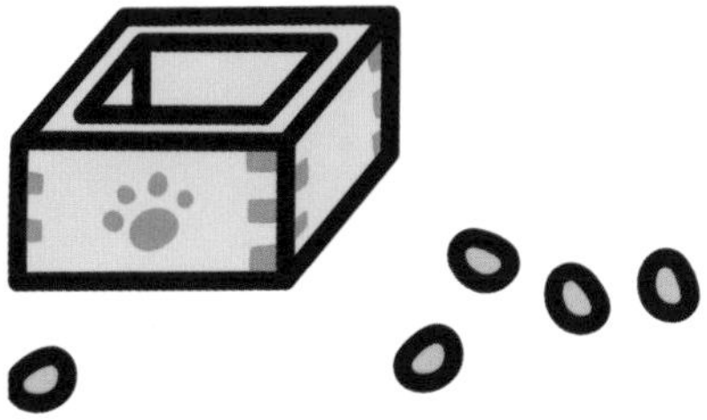

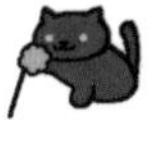

Surprise, I'm hungry!
Yummy meat treats now, meow?
Kitty kitty please?!

Chocolate fish with bow…

Will you be my Valentine?

Meant for each other.

FEBRUARY: Fish Jump through Cracked Ice

Family album—
Collect pics of cute kitties.
Where are they meow?!

Beside the rose-gold
Pussy willow the kitty's
Tail thrashes quickly.

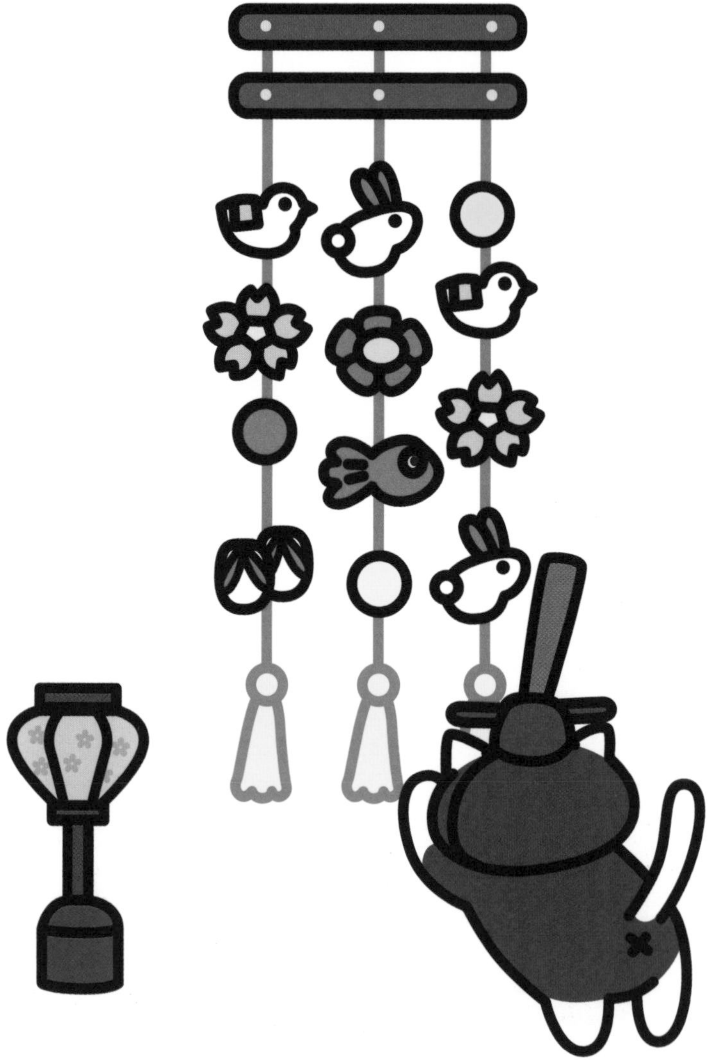

Princess for a day…?

Kitties are always royal.

Obey my meow!

MARCH: Plants Send up Tender Shoots

On a warm spring day
Three kitties play with their toys
Purr and roll and purr.

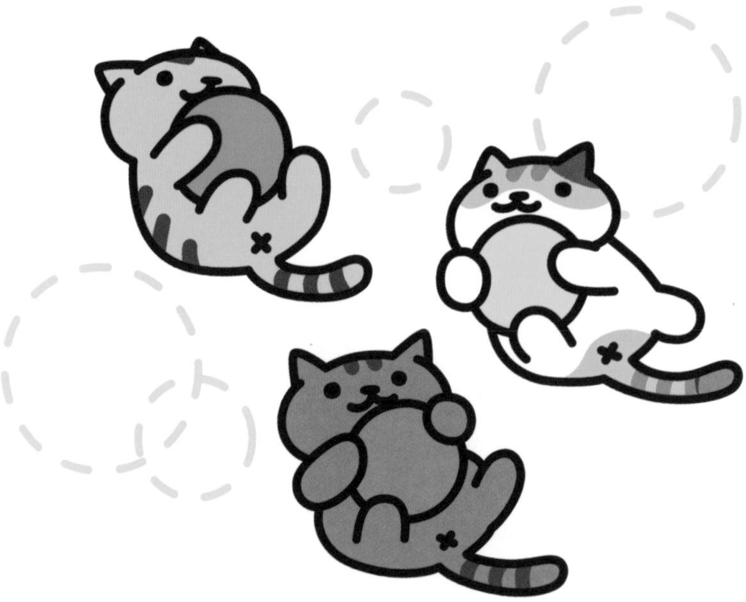

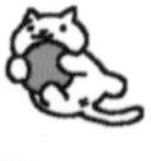

Another spring day…
Flower yellow like the sun
Warms me as I nap.

MARCH: Peach Trees Blossom

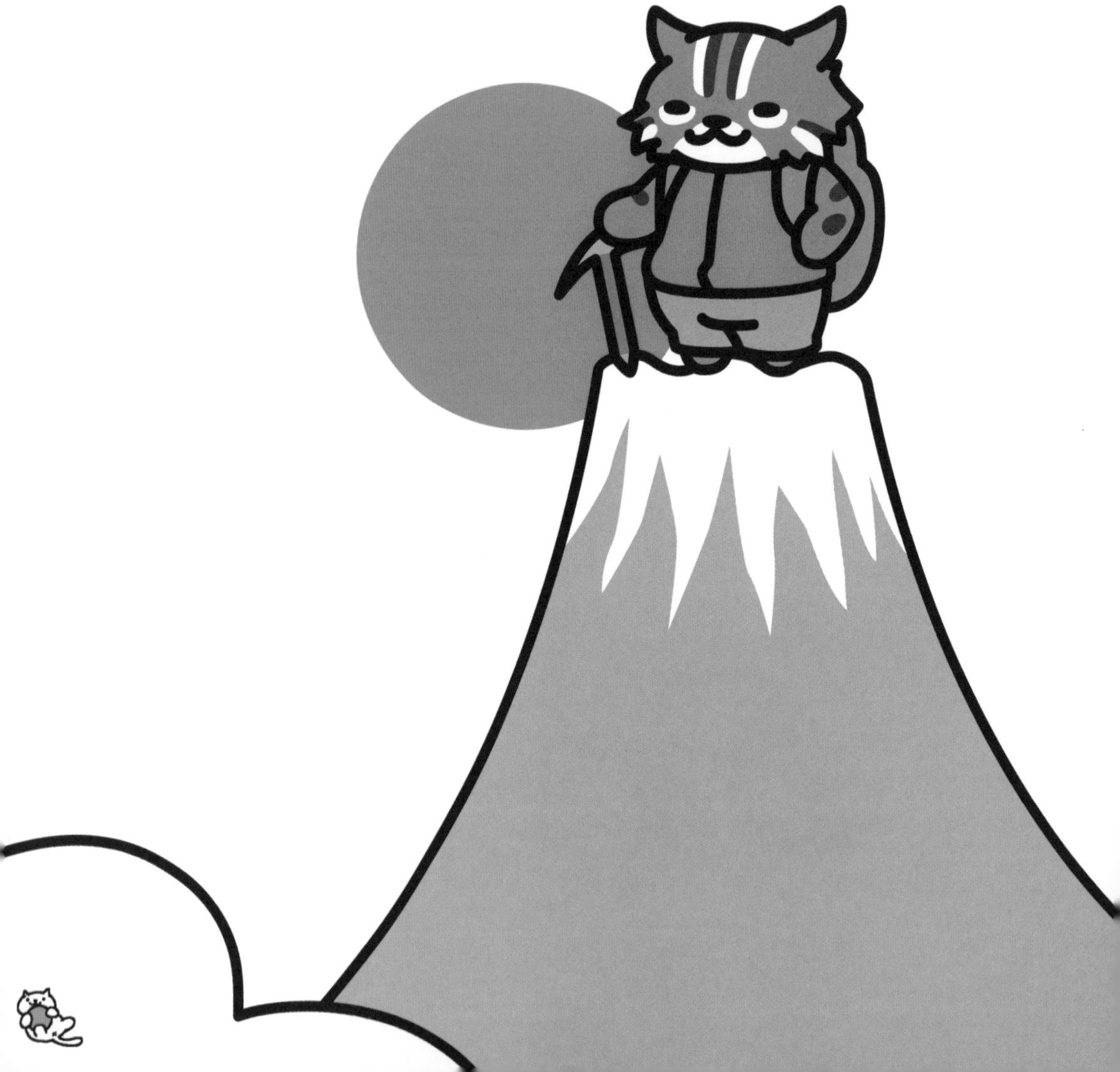

Climbed up the mountain
To conquer the world below.
Clouds beneath my feet.

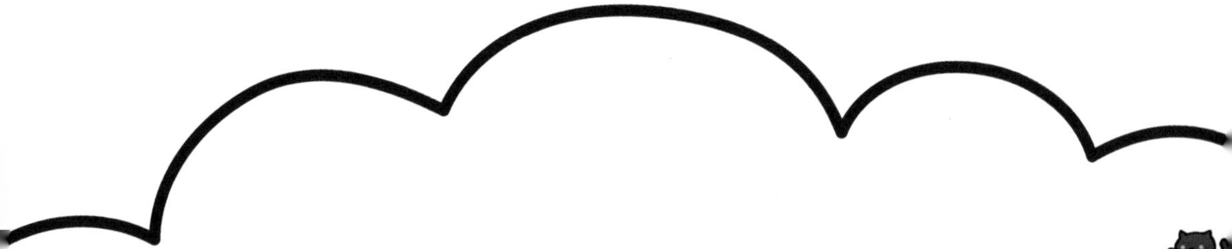

In the soft spring breeze
Flowers sway on slender stalks.
Kitty love will bloom.

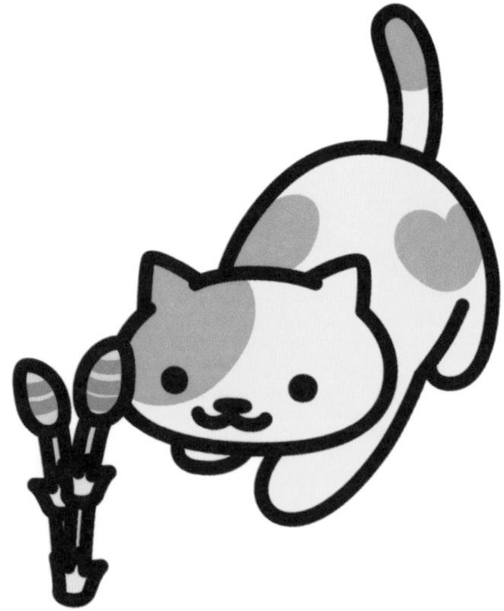

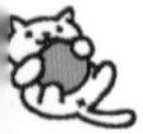

Mochi-shaped cushion—
I might eat it in my dreams
Nom and on and nom.

MARCH: Cherry Trees Blossom

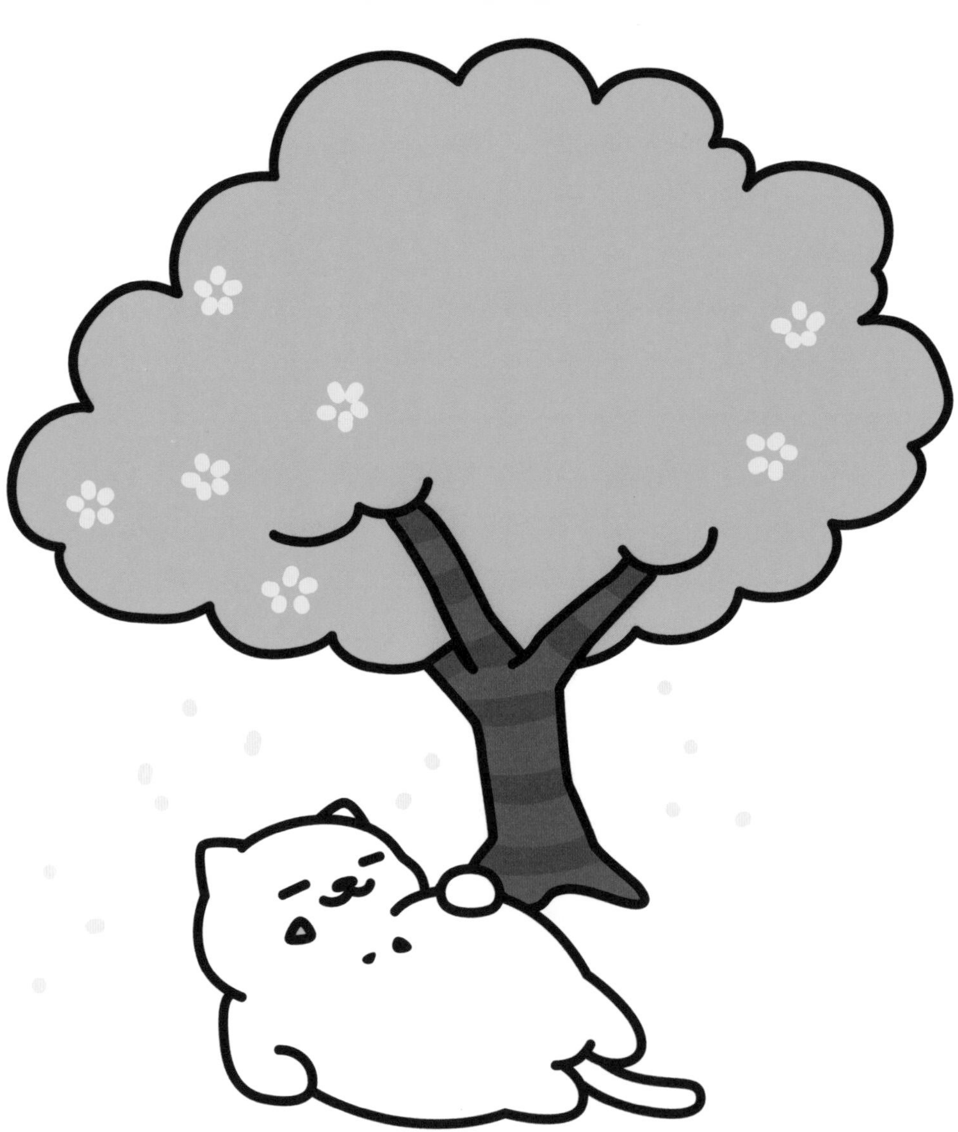

Life is so tasty!
Tummy blossoms before me,
Cherry tree above.

MARCH: Thunder Rolls In

Board the Spring Express!
Full speed ahead down the track...
All kitties are go!

APRIL: Swallows Return

Packing up to move…
Happy kitty in the box
Will have to move too.

The picnic basket
Is waiting for you to come
And carry it home.

APRIL: Rainbows Appear

Pussyfoot outside
With me to pick some tender
Wild vegetables.

We went out to fish.

I ate everything we caught.

I have no regrets.

APRIL: Frosts End and Seedlings Sprout

Heat wave party time!
This kitty needs a cool fan
And more fans beneath.

APRIL: Peonies Bloom

Kitty File 1

Solid White

Snowball

MY KITTY'S NAME IS

PERSONALITY | Mellow

♥ favorite goodies
1
2
3

80

KITTY
no.01

Solid Black

Smokey

MY KITTY'S NAME IS

PERSONALITY | Hot and Cold

♥ favorite goodies
1
2
3

140

KITTY
no.02

Black & White

Spots

MY KITTY'S NAME IS

PERSONALITY | Joker

♥ favorite goodies
1
2
3

75

KITTY
no.03

Solid Grey

Shadow

MY KITTY'S NAME IS

PERSONALITY | Peculiar

♥ favorite goodies
1
2
3

50

KITTY
no.04

Turkish Calico

Sunny

MY KITTY'S NAME IS

PERSONALITY | Mischievous

❤ favorite goodies

1

2

3

120

KITTY no.05

Orange Tabby

Fred

MY KITTY'S NAME IS

PERSONALITY | Lady-Killer

❤ favorite goodies

1

2

3

150

KITTY no.06

Orange & White Tabby

Pumpkin

MY KITTY'S NAME IS

PERSONALITY | Spacey

❤ favorite goodies

1

2

3

90

KITTY no.07

Calico

Callie

MY KITTY'S NAME IS

PERSONALITY | Carefree

❤ favorite goodies

1

2

3

50

KITTY no.08

Rare Kitty File 1

28

Baseball Jersey

RARE KITTY
no.01

Joe DiMeowgio

MY KITTY'S NAME IS

PERSONALITY | Team Player

♥ memo

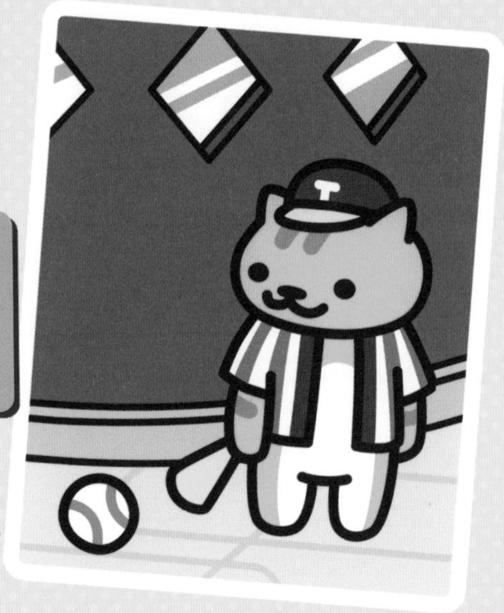

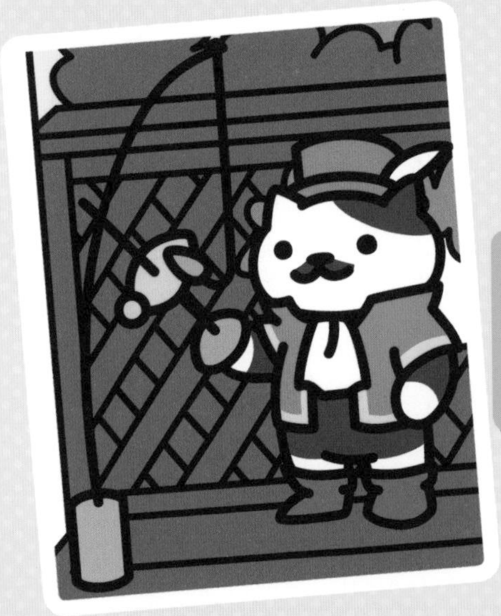

30

Mustachioed

RARE KITTY
no.02

Señor Don Gato

MY KITTY'S NAME IS

PERSONALITY | Scheming

♥ memo

70

Persian

RARE KITTY

no.03

Xerxes IX

MY KITTY'S NAME IS

PERSONALITY | Regal

♥ memo

111

Camouflage

RARE KITTY

no.04

Chairman Meow

MY KITTY'S NAME IS

PERSONALITY | Boorish

♥ memo

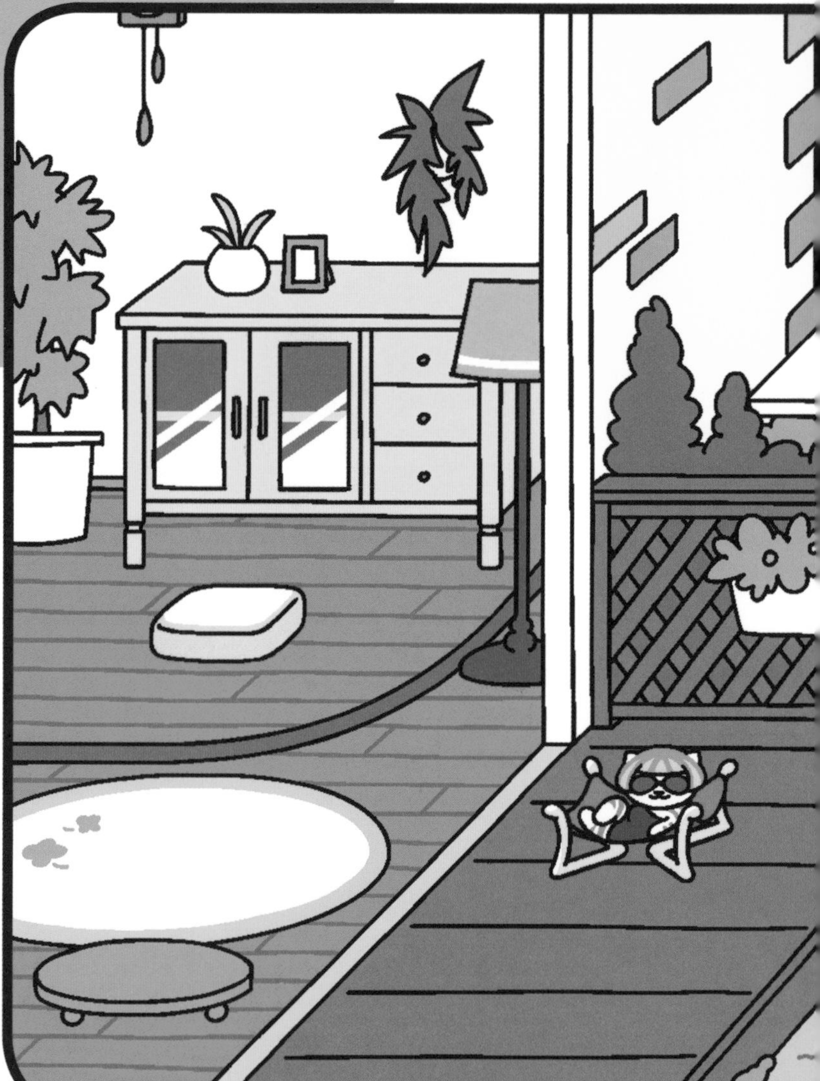

SUMMER

Things are backward when
Fish eat fluffy kitty cats,
But these are tunnels.

MAY: Frogs Begin to Croak

I'm a stray kitty,
This carnation is for my
Lost mama kitty.

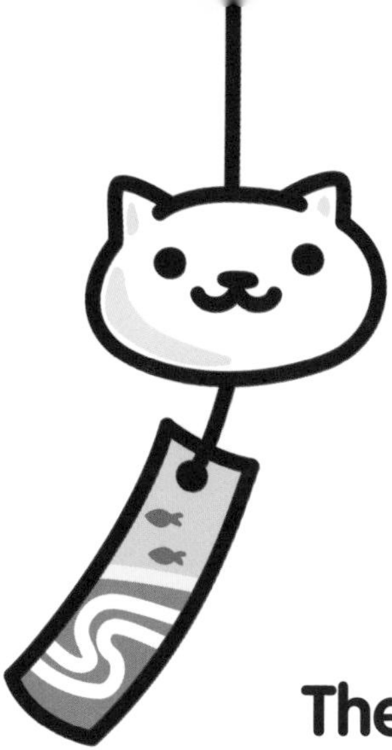

The summer breeze wafts
A delicate scent to me—
The smell of sardines.

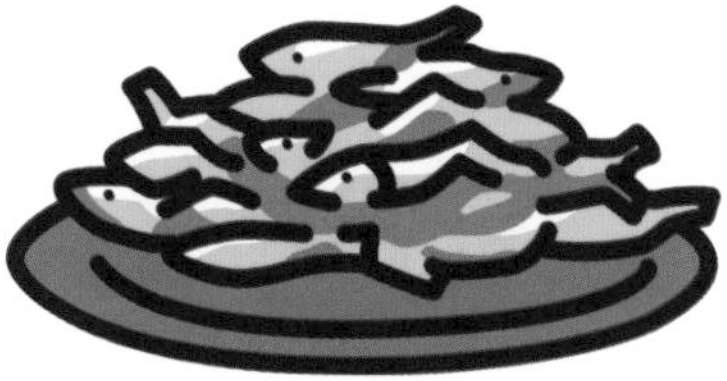

Paws uplifted to

The cerulean May sky—

Purr with ecstasy.

On the summer breeze—
Kitty sways in the hammock,
The scent of cut grass.

MAY: Safflowers Bloom

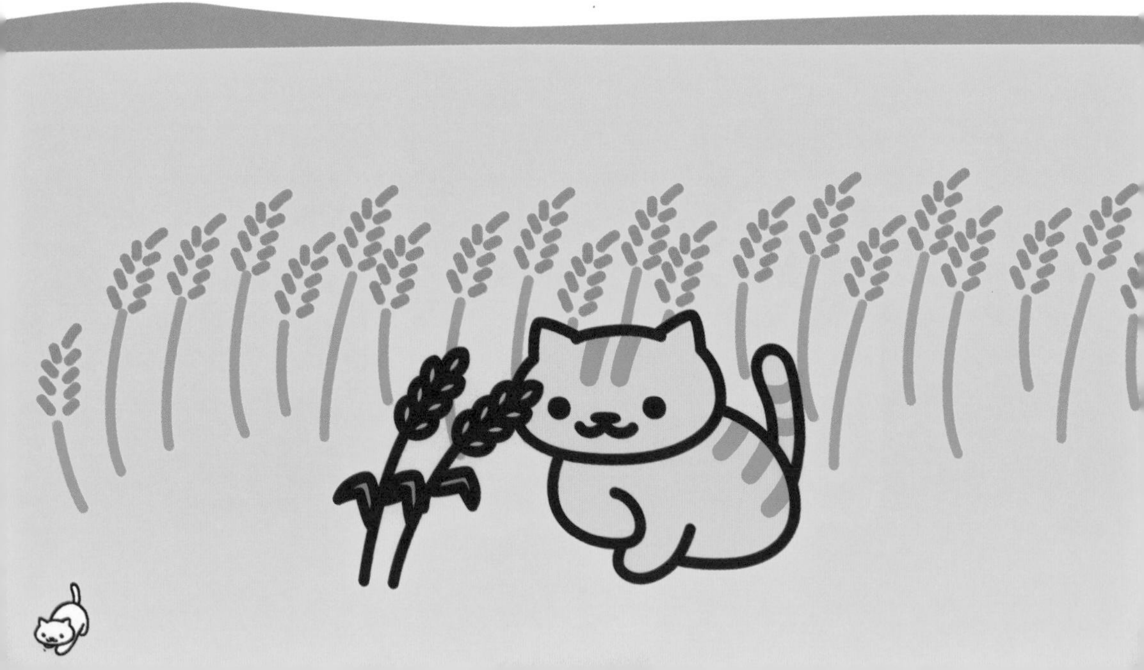

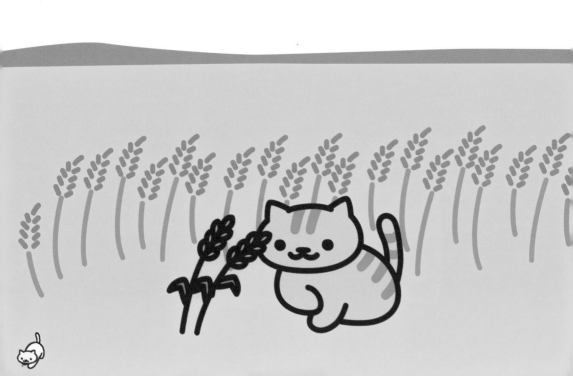

When stalks of wheat sway,
Curious kitty observes,
Then paw swats, swats, swats.

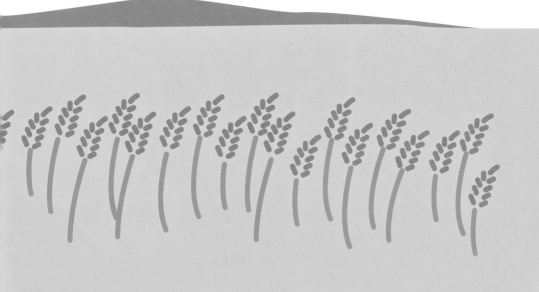

There's no way that I
Will go on a diet or
Fit into that thing.

JUNE: Praying Mantises Emerge

Hiding in the dark,
A flickering light betrays…
Kitty or fireflies?

Fill crocks with plum jam?
No room. They are preserving
Kitties jammed inside.

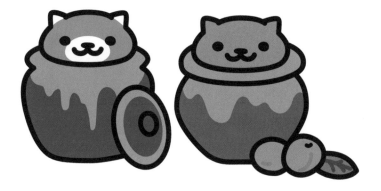

JUNE: Mirabelle Plums Turn Yellow

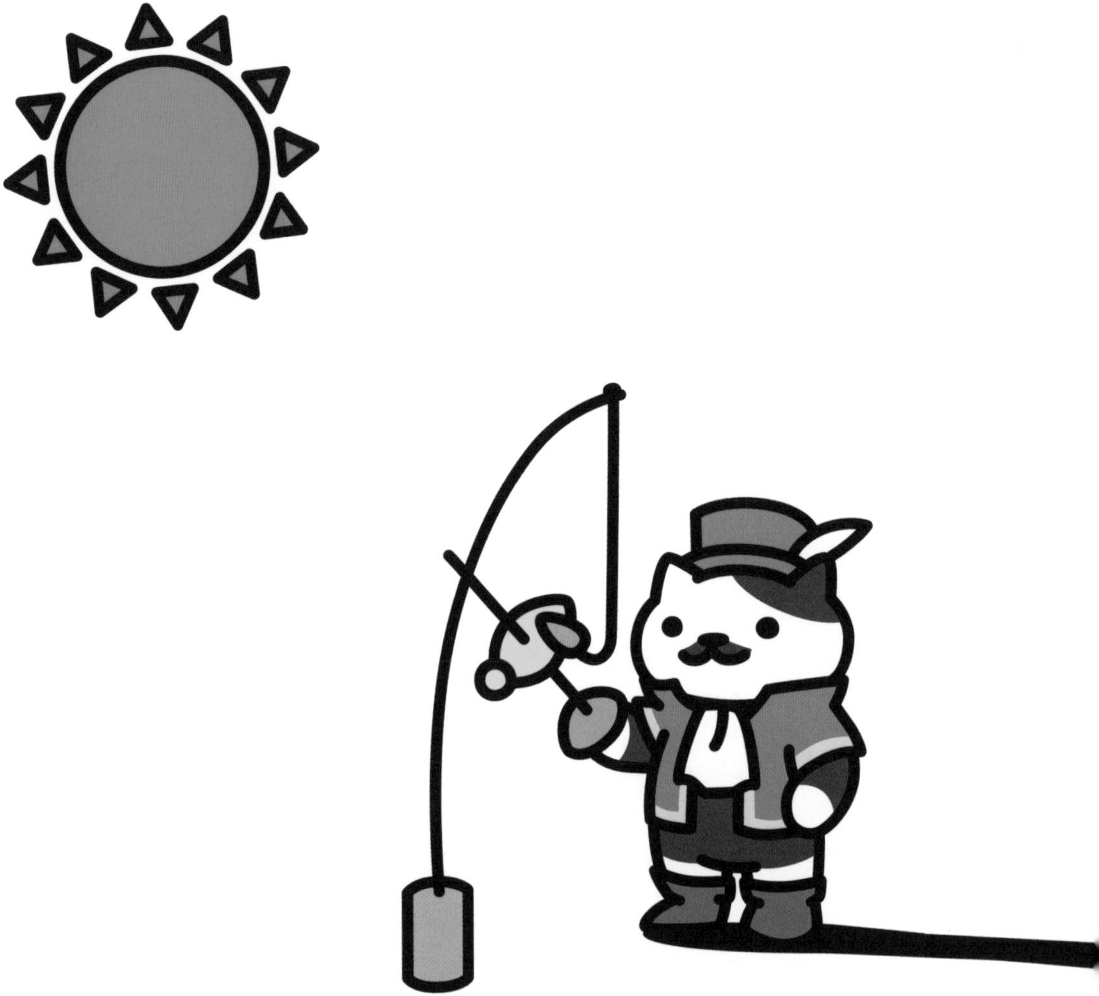

Hunting and fishing

On an endless summer day,

Casting my own shade.

JUNE: Self-Heal Withers

Meow, it's thunder!
Hide inside the cardboard box
Before lightning strikes!

Swimming season starts.
Trying to catch a fish lunch,
Kitty dives right in.

JULY: Crow-Dipper Grows

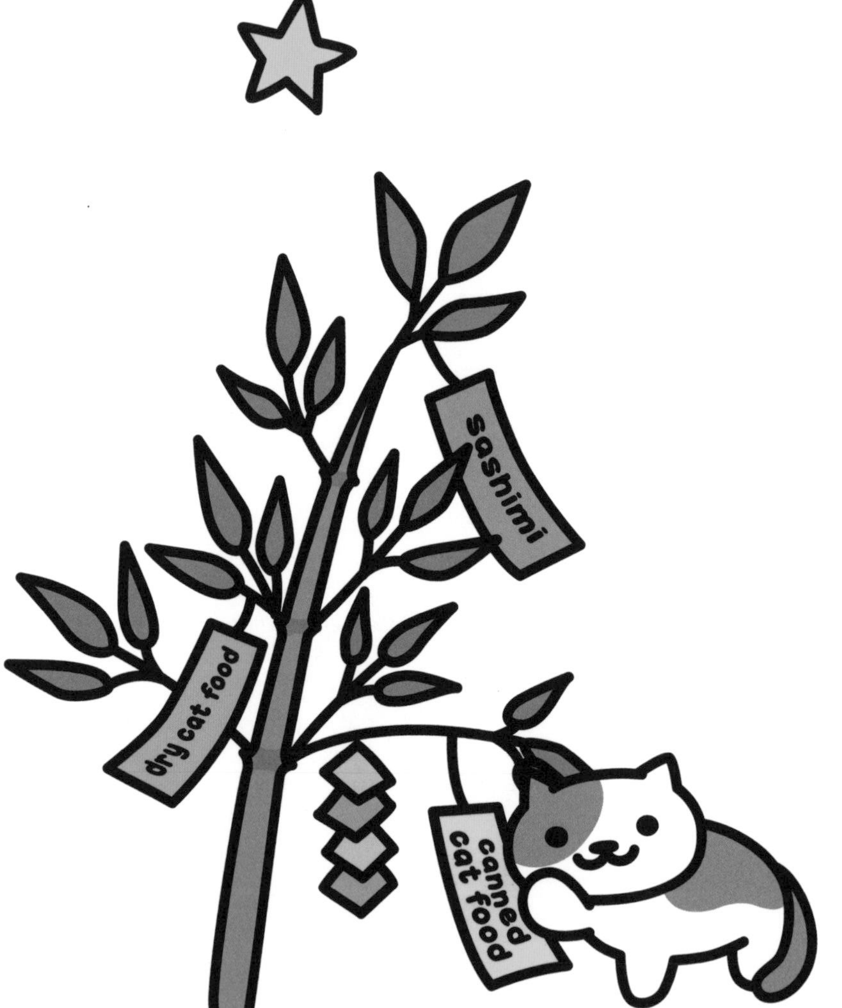
sashimi
dry cat food
canned
cat food

The Star Festival—

Tied to bamboo, my wishes

Are for more fishes.

Making faces at
The four-legged veggie stools…
Which one will laugh first?

My summer retreat—
Via my flying carpet
I will chill there soon.

JULY: Hawks Fledge

Now can you spot how
Many spotted kitties are
In the spotted tube?

Tropical sunbeams

Sunning me in my hammock—

Vacation meow.

On a scorching day,

Even kitties can't resist

Cool water bucket.

AUGUST: Cloudbursts

Kitty File 2

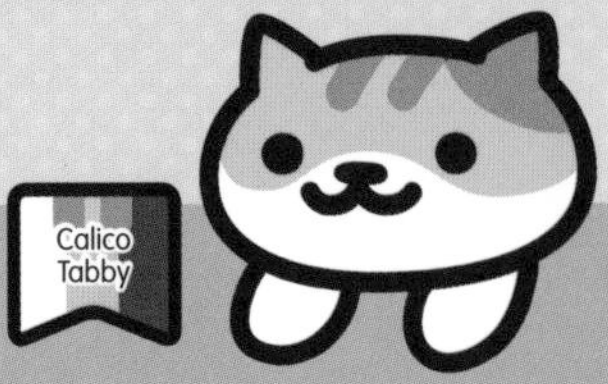
Calico Tabby

Tabitha

MY KITTY'S NAME IS

PERSONALITY | Leisurely

♥ favorite goodies

1

2

3

40

KITTY no.09

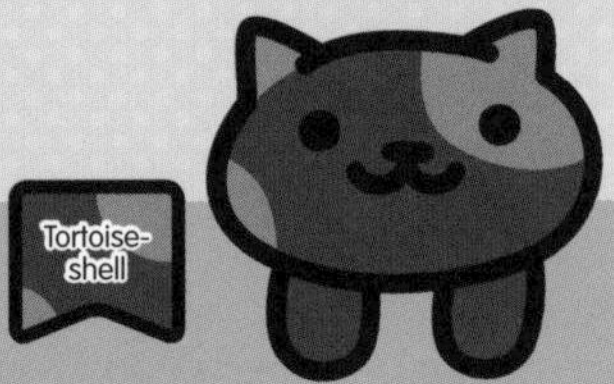
Tortoise-shell

Bandit

MY KITTY'S NAME IS

PERSONALITY | Wild at Heart

♥ favorite goodies

1

2

3

180

KITTY no.10

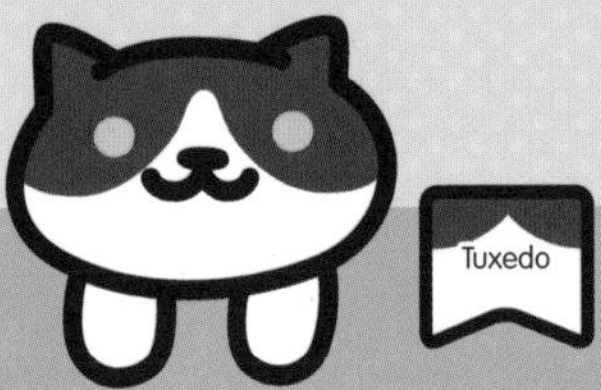
Tuxedo

Gabriel

MY KITTY'S NAME IS

PERSONALITY | Diligent

♥ favorite goodies

1

2

3

150

KITTY no.11

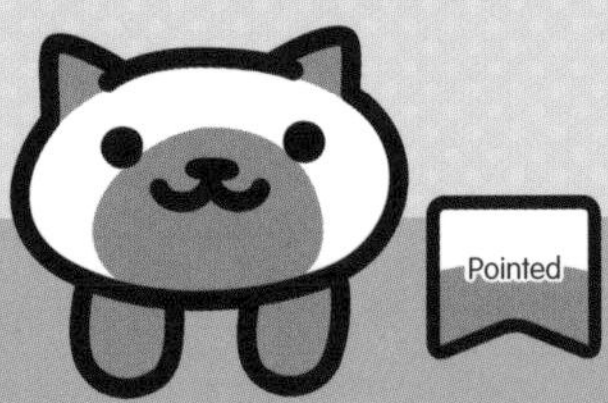
Pointed

Marshmallow

MY KITTY'S NAME IS

PERSONALITY | Aloof

♥ favorite goodies

1

2

3

170

KITTY no.12

Black with White Mitts

Socks

MY KITTY'S NAME IS

PERSONALITY | Adventurous

♥ favorite goodies

1

2

3

70

KITTY

no.13

Grey & White

Lexy

MY KITTY'S NAME IS

PERSONALITY | Expensive Tastes

♥ favorite goodies

1

2

3

100

KITTY

no.14

Brown Tabby

Bolt

MY KITTY'S NAME IS

PERSONALITY | Insatiable

♥ favorite goodies

1

2

3

140

KITTY

no.15

Brown & White Tabby

Breezy

MY KITTY'S NAME IS

PERSONALITY | Laid-Back

♥ favorite goodies

1

2

3

30

KITTY

no.16

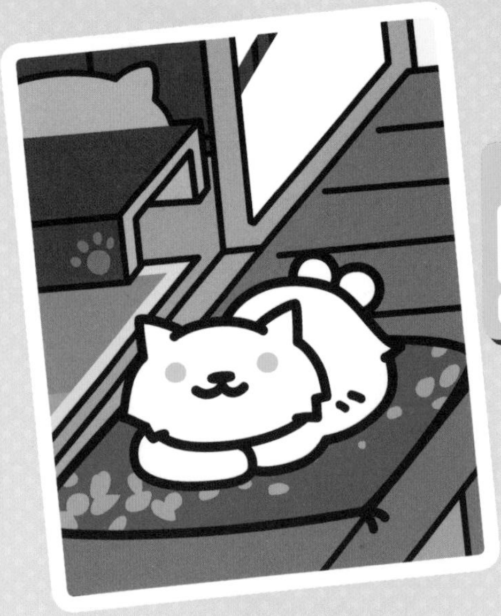

222

Ethereal

RARE KITTY
no.05

Saint Purrtrick

MY KITTY'S NAME IS

PERSONALITY | Awe-Inspiring

♥ memo

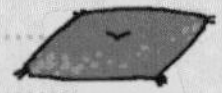

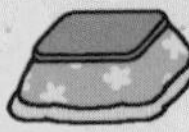

20

Gold

RARE KITTY
no.06

Ms. Fortune

MY KITTY'S NAME IS

PERSONALITY | Charismatic

♥ memo

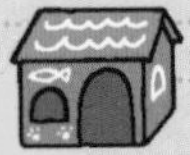

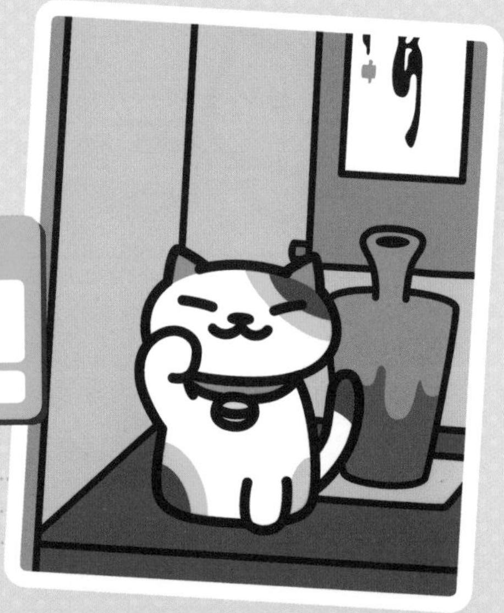

Adventurer

40
RARE KITTY
no.07

Bob the Cat

MY KITTY'S NAME IS

PERSONALITY | Outdoorsy

♥ memo
....
....
....

Railway Uniform

50
RARE KITTY
no.08

Conductor Whiskers

MY KITTY'S NAME IS

PERSONALITY | Vigilant

♥ memo
....
....

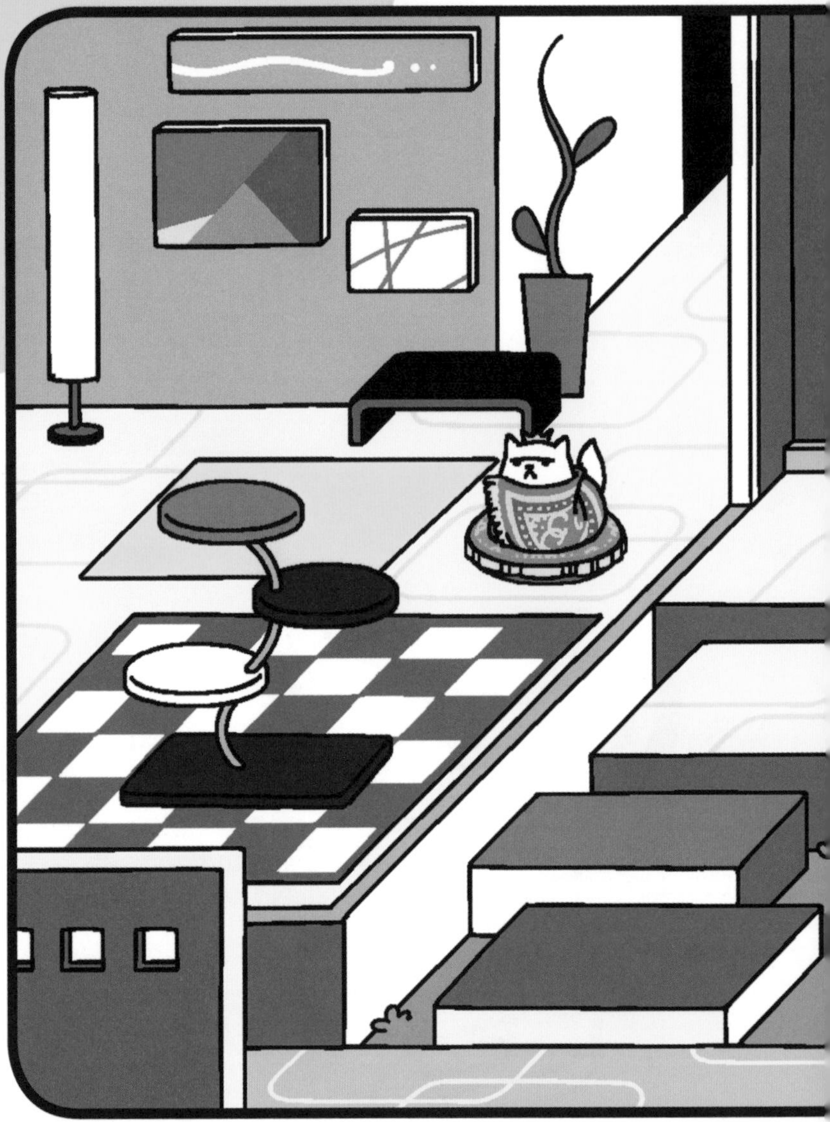

AUTUMN

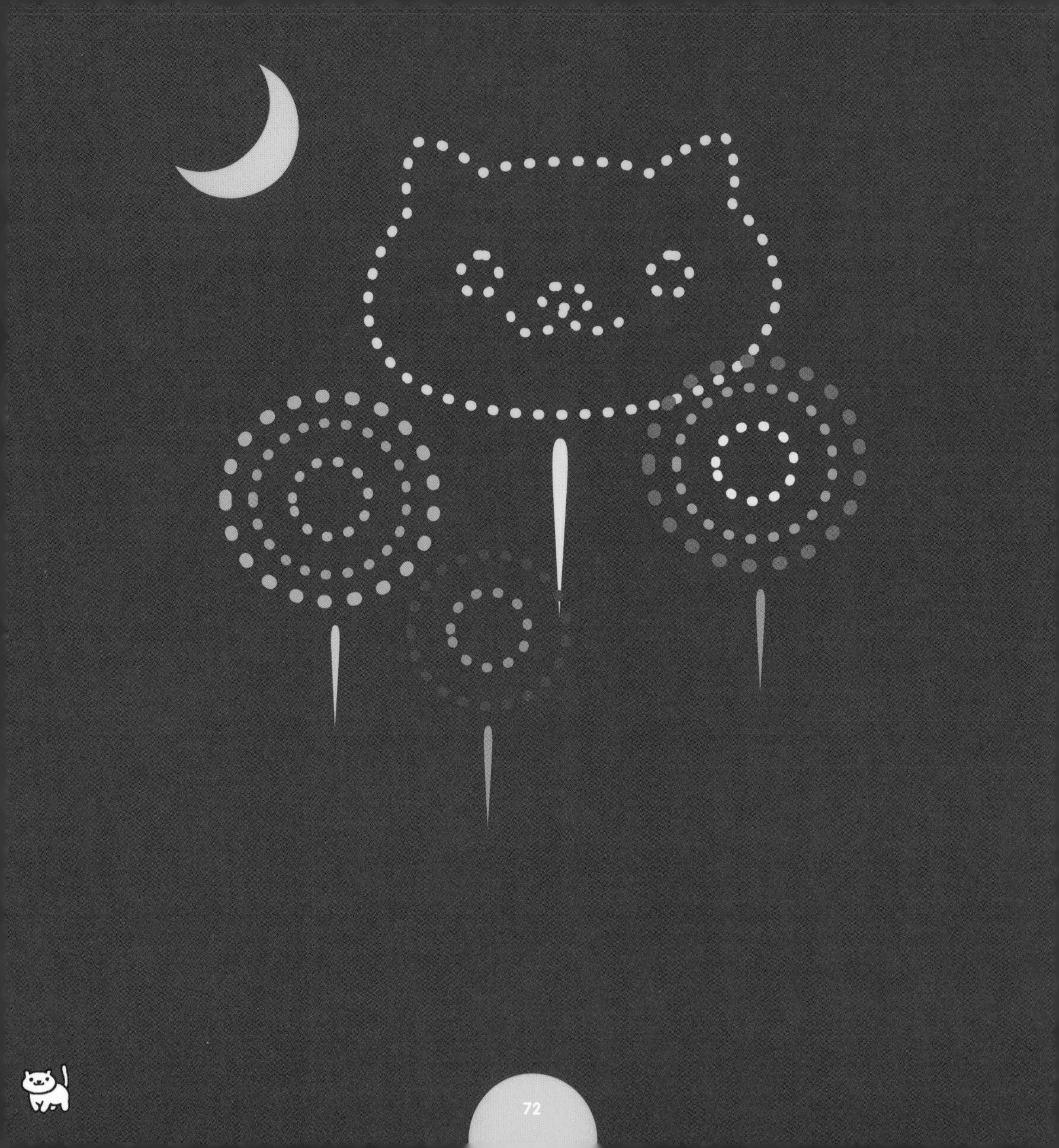

Cooler August nights…
Exploding into the sky—
One kitty firework.

AUGUST: Breezes Blow

Sitting on the porch
Drinking milk and moon gazing…
What does it all mean?

Just watching the fish
You caught at the carnival!
Wolf in sheep's clothing...

On the empty beach
A single shell earring lost
And found by kitty.

AUGUST: Cotton Bolls Split Open

Summer vacation!
Play and have lots of fun but
No sunburn for me.

The proud hunter brings
Dinner à la carte for you—
Crunchy cicada.

SEPTEMBER: Rice Sheaves Ripen

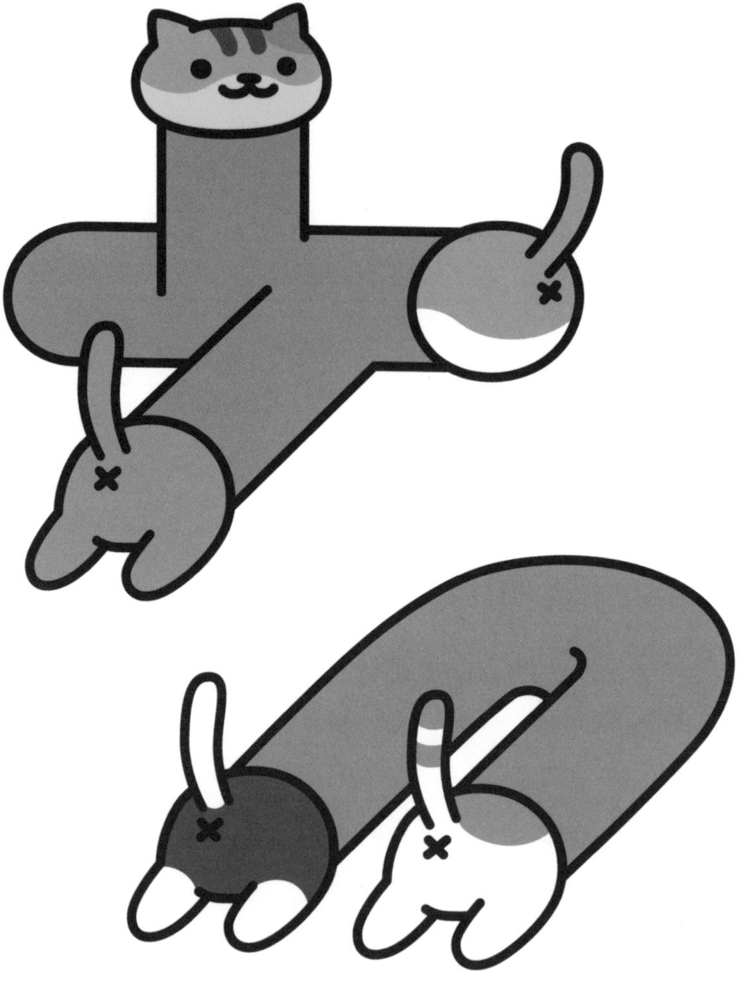

Ready, set, go! Find my
Soft tail waving to and fro...
Kitty hide-and-seek.

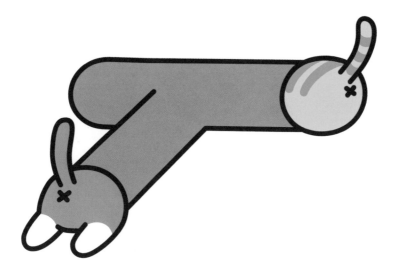

SEPTEMBER: Dew Sparkles on Grass

It's meowy comfy
On five red silk crepe pillows
Living my nine lives.

Mister Dragonfly!
Crouch, jump, catch it in the air
Under blue fall skies.

Green Tail-Thing Teaser—
Pretend it's a blade of grass.
Admire its beauty.

It's almost ready…
Making pizza garnished with
A Kick Toy Saury.

SEPTEMBER: Insects Burrow into the Ground to Hibernate

**Time to put away
Summer clothes. Which coat would you
Like to grow meow?**

OCTOBER: Rice Paddy Fields Are Drained

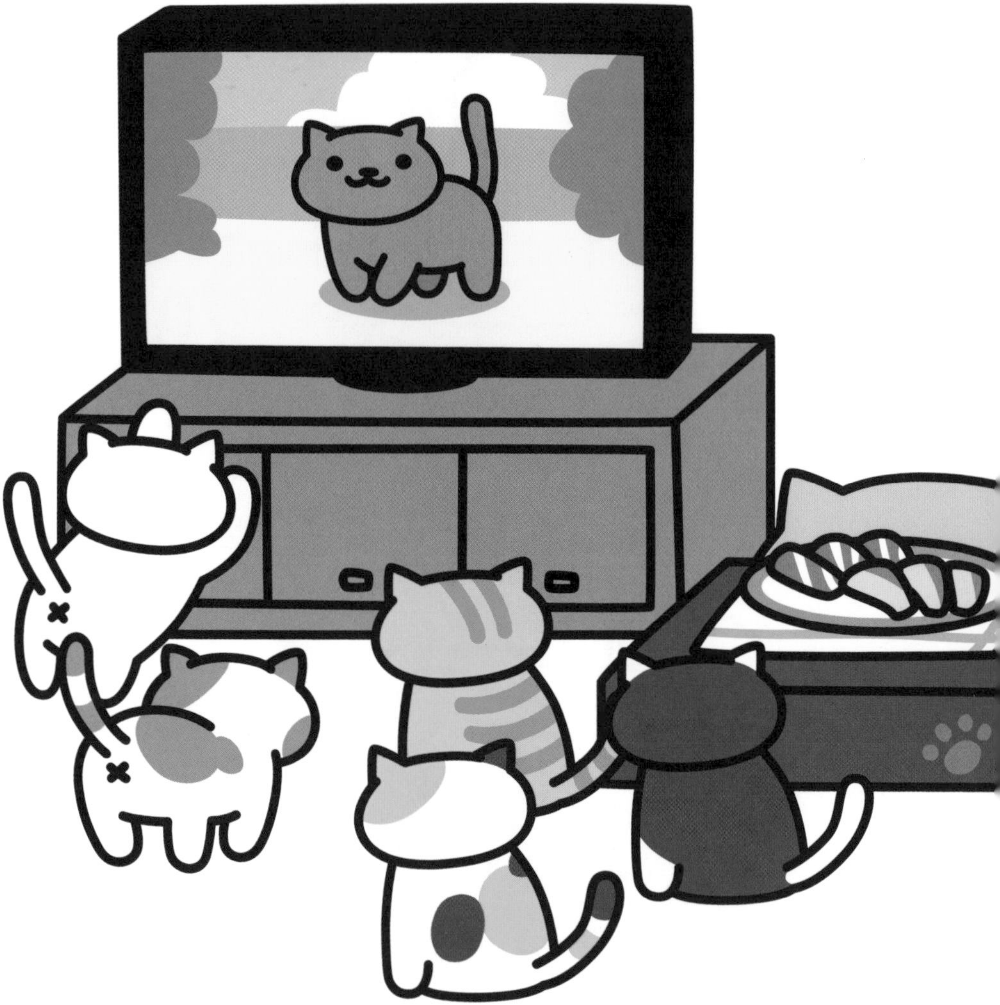

One by one they come,

On a cool crisp autumn night—

Kitty conference.

OCTOBER: Geese Arrive

Ready, set, go…scratch!
In this odd competition
The upholstery wins.

It's the World Series!
Can Joe DiMeowgio score
A home run for us?

OCTOBER: Crickets Sing in Doorways

A smooth, sharp acorn!
I will hide it deep inside
My bag of treasures.

This Halloween what
Should kitty transform into?
Magical kitty.

OCTOBER: Gentle Rain Showers Fall

Fall leaves are turning!
Let's drive our small cardboard truck
Into the meow-tains.

NOVEMBER: Maple Leaves and Grapevines Turn Colors

Kitty File 3

Misty

Mackerel Tabby

MY KITTY'S NAME IS

PERSONALITY | Lazy

♥ favorite goodies
1
2
3

160

KITTY no.17

Pickles

Gray & White Tabby

MY KITTY'S NAME IS

PERSONALITY | Fainthearted

♥ favorite goodies
1
2
3

○

KITTY no.18

Pepper

Black with Odd Eyes

MY KITTY'S NAME IS

PERSONALITY | Shy

♥ favorite goodies
1
2
3

165

KITTY no.19

Patches

Orange Patches

MY KITTY'S NAME IS

PERSONALITY | Jealous

♥ favorite goodies
1
2
3

80

KITTY no.20

Gozer

Tortoise-shell Tabby

MY KITTY'S NAME IS

PERSONALITY | Sore Loser

♥ **favorite goodies**
1
2
3

155

KITTY
no.21

Cocoa

Brown Tuxedo

MY KITTY'S NAME IS

PERSONALITY | Indecisive

♥ **favorite goodies**
1
2
3

45

KITTY
no.22

Princess

Striped Torbie

MY KITTY'S NAME IS

PERSONALITY | Ditzy

♥ **favorite goodies**
1
2
3

125

KITTY
no.23

Ginger

Red with White Mitts

MY KITTY'S NAME IS

PERSONALITY | Bashful

♥ **favorite goodies**
1
2
3

60

KITTY
no.24

Rare Kitty File 3

250

Ronin

RARE KITTY
no.09

Mr. Meowgi

MY KITTY'S NAME IS

PERSONALITY | Mentoring

♥ memo

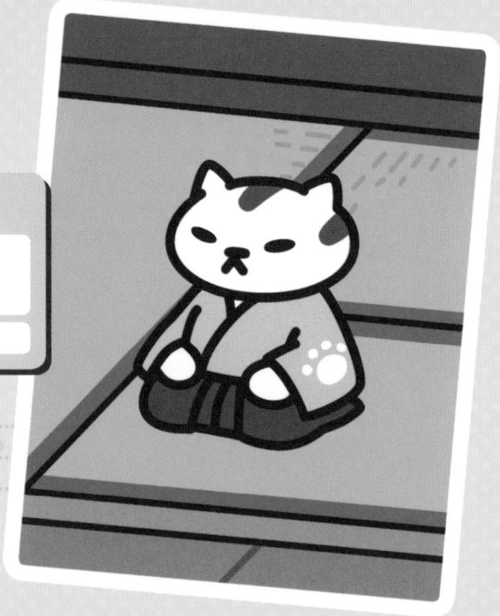

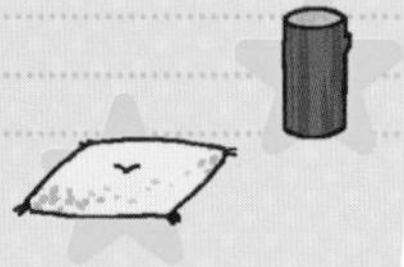

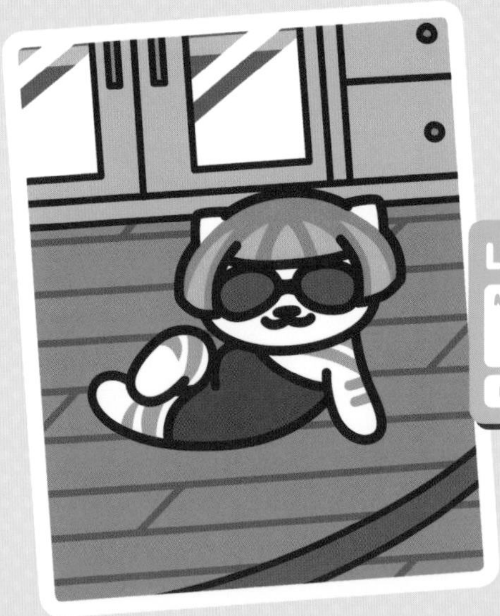

100

American Shorthair

RARE KITTY
no.10

Lady Meow-Meow

MY KITTY'S NAME IS

PERSONALITY | Diva

♥ memo

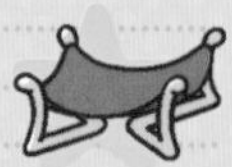

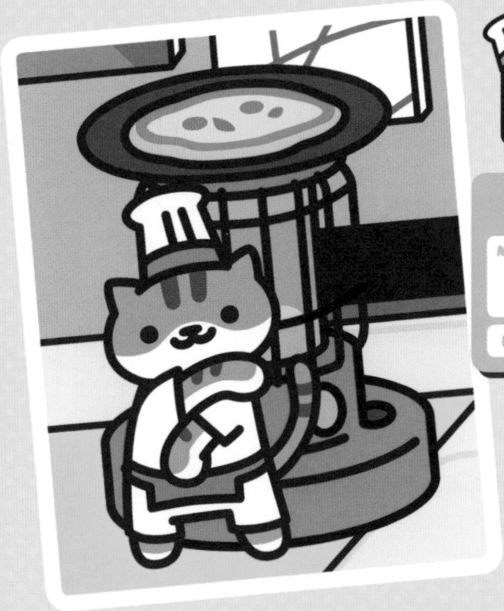

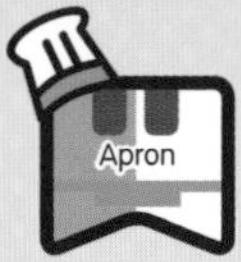
Apron

30

RARE KITTY

no.11

Guy Furry

MY KITTY'S NAME IS

PERSONALITY | Artisan

♥ memo

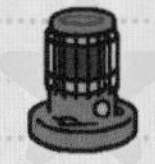

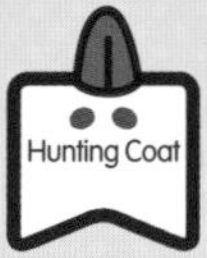
Hunting Coat

150

RARE KITTY

no.12

Kathmandu

MY KITTY'S NAME IS

PERSONALITY | Refined

♥ memo

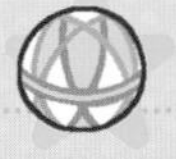

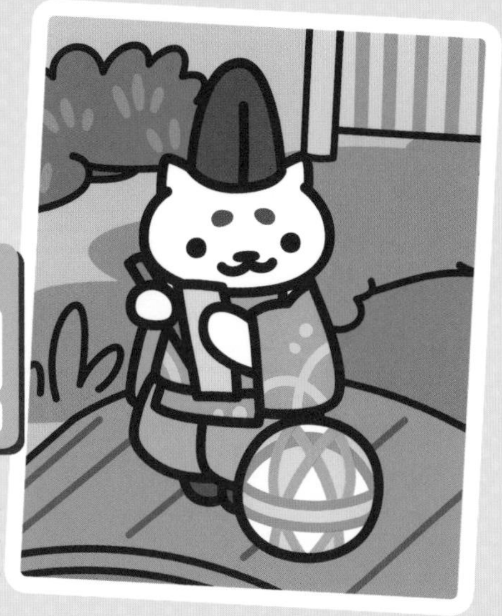

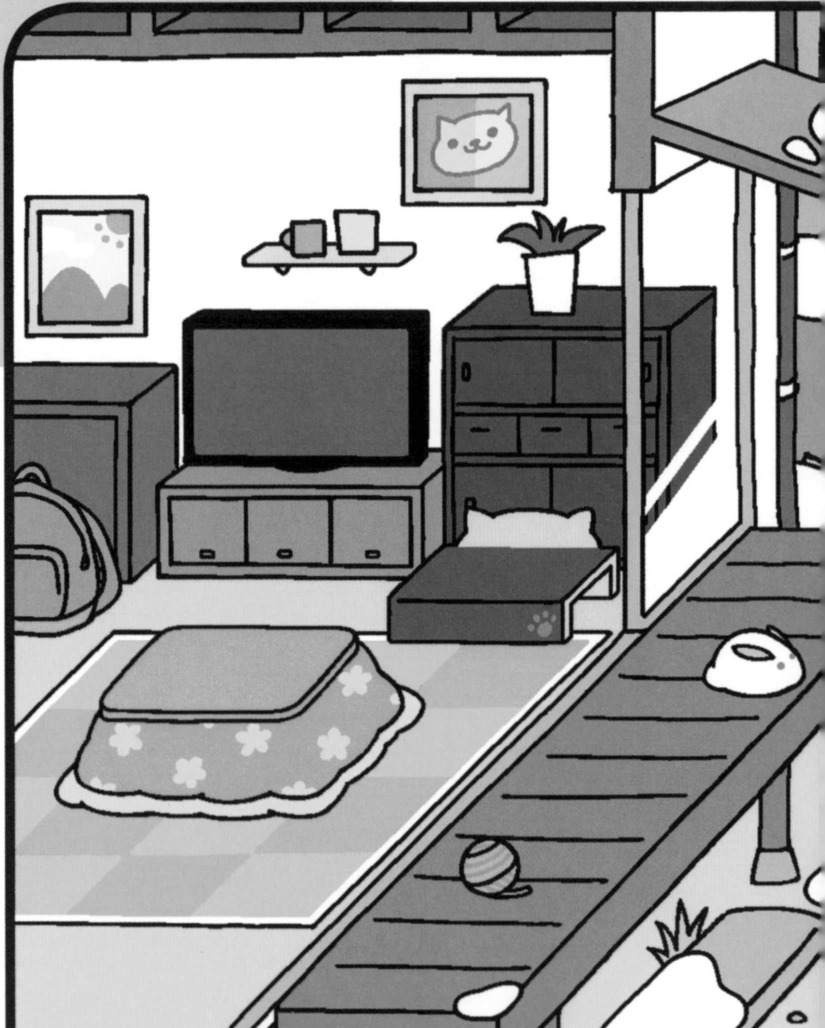

WINTER

Fish-stick tunnel cats,
You should be eating fish sticks
Not the other way 'round!

Each piece has a face.
When you slice, this candy roll
Keeps coming up cats.

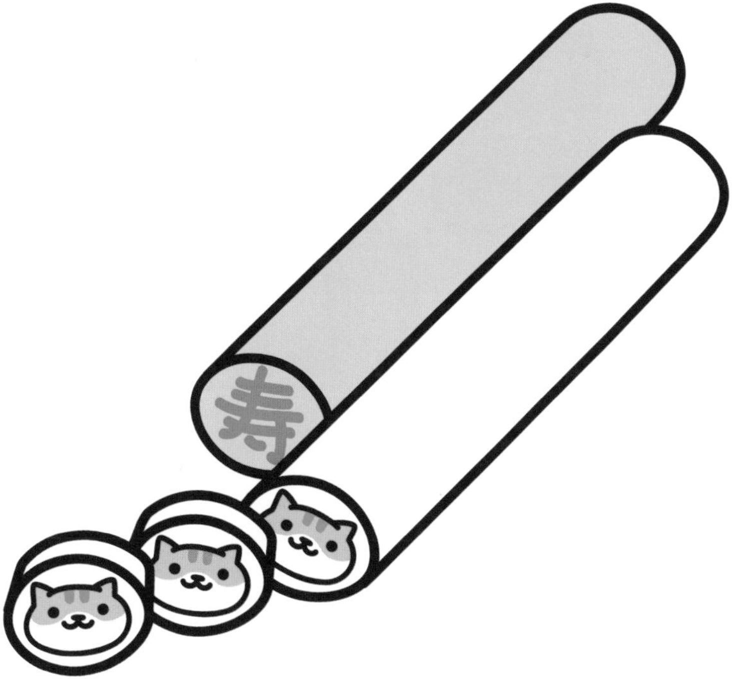
寿

Kitty ornament

Decorating your shop's door

Rakes in good fortune.

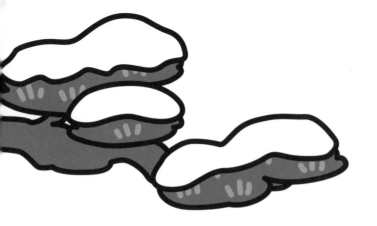

On fresh fallen snow
A set of tracks left behind—
Small kitty blossoms.

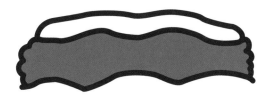

NOVEMBER: Rainbows Hide behind Clouds

On snowy days too
We must train in the way of
Kitty samurai.

Fluffy, cozy, warm—
Enemies become close friends
When it's cold outside.

DECEMBER: Tachibana Oranges Turn Yellow

Kitty hot pot chef

Says, "Eat it while it's hot!" but

I won't burn my tongue!

DECEMBER: The Sun Hides and Winter Arrives

First, I make biscuits…
Then, I need a long winter's nap
On my kneaded bed.

It seems I'm sorry

For all the mischief this year,

But I'm just napping.

DECEMBER: Salmon Run up Rivers

Dear Santa Claus, please
Fill up our stockings. We have
Been hung up with care.

New Year's cleaning time!
Quit playing with your toy ball
And lend us a paw.

DECEMBER: Deer Shed Their Antlers

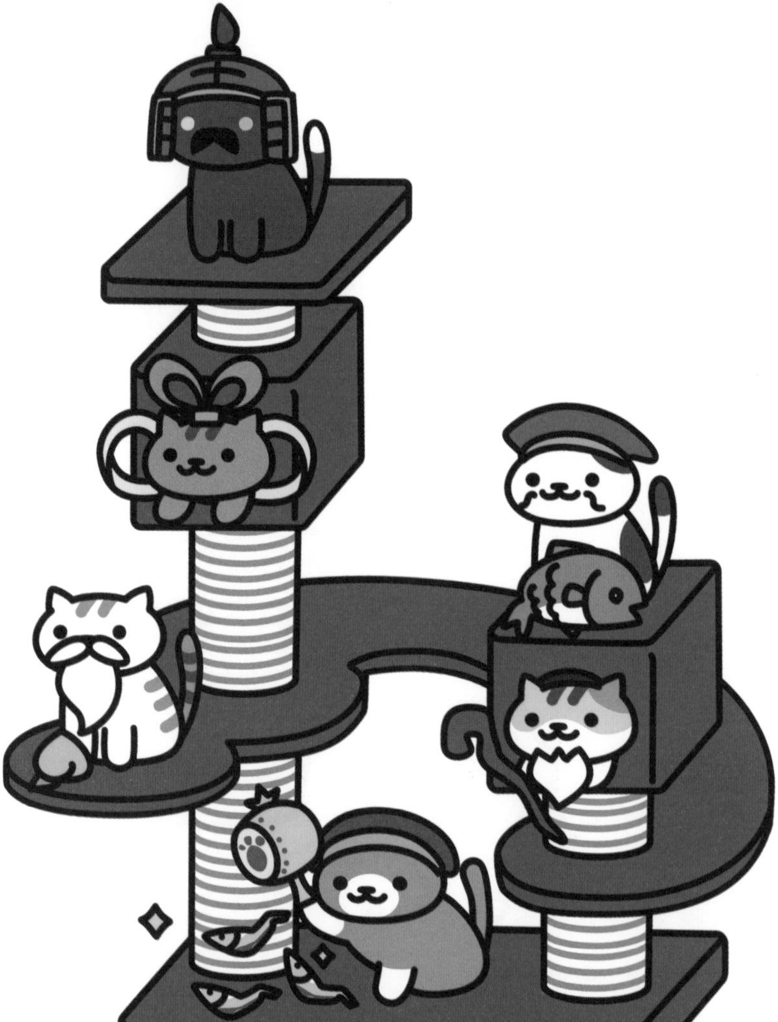

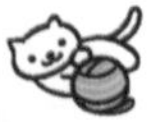

Japanese good luck—
Seven Gods of Fortune perch
On the cat tower.

JANUARY: Wheat Sprouts Break through the Snow

Let's write all of our
New Year's resolutions in
The form of haiku!

JANUARY: Japanese Parsley Burgeons

Mochi with orange.

True, I am disguised as one…

But please don't eat me!

People live longer,

But when cats get to twenty

They become magic!

JANUARY: Pheasants Begin to Sing

Another cold day
Under the warm kotatsu—
A kitty hot spot.

JANUARY: Bog Rhubarb Buds

When it snows a lot,
My dome becomes an igloo.
Cool, right? But it's warm!

As the snow softly
Falls I fall into a deep
Sleep in my soft bed.

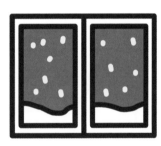

JANUARY: Hens Begin to Lay Eggs

Kitty File 4

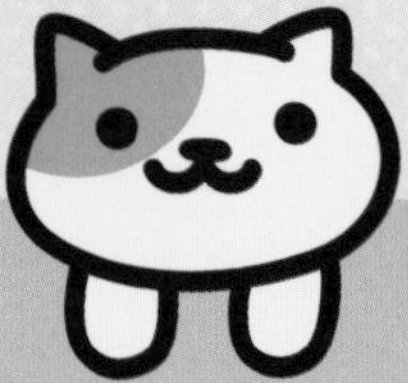

Tan & Orange

Peaches

MY KITTY'S NAME IS

PERSONALITY | Capricious

♥ favorite goodies

1

2

3

45

KITTY no.25

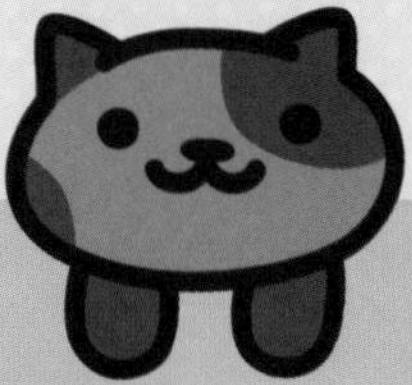

Red Tortoise-shell

Spud

MY KITTY'S NAME IS

PERSONALITY | Cautious

♥ favorite goodies

1

2

3

80

KITTY no.26

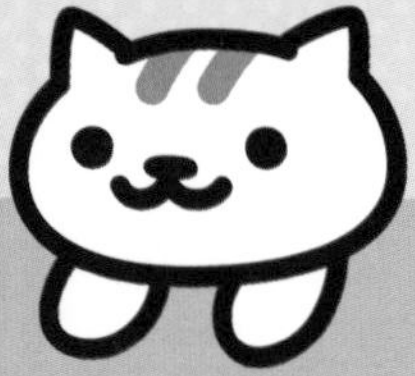

White Mackerel

Mack

MY KITTY'S NAME IS

PERSONALITY | Determined

♥ favorite goodies

1

2

3

130

KITTY no.27

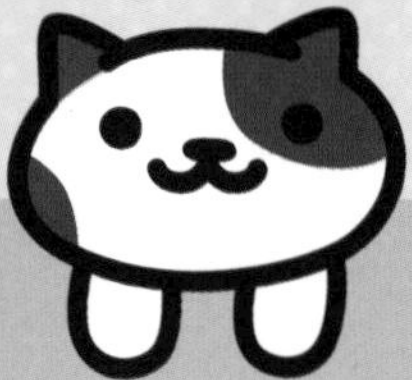

Black Patches

Speckles

MY KITTY'S NAME IS

PERSONALITY | Lonely

♥ favorite goodies

1

2

3

40

KITTY no.28

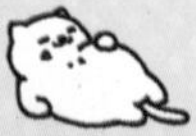

Rare Kitty File 4

Tubbs

MY KITTY'S NAME IS

PERSONALITY | Finicky Feaster

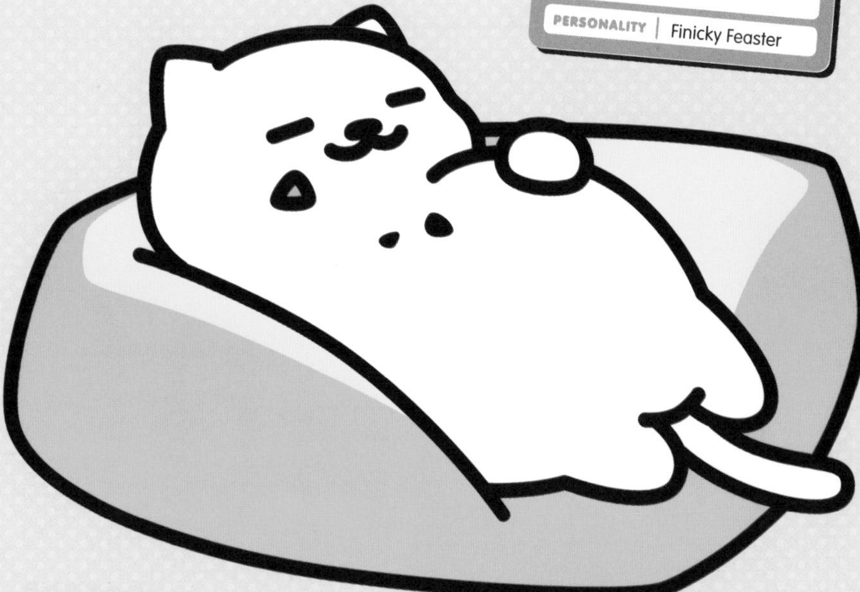

130

Fluffy

RARE KITTY
no.13

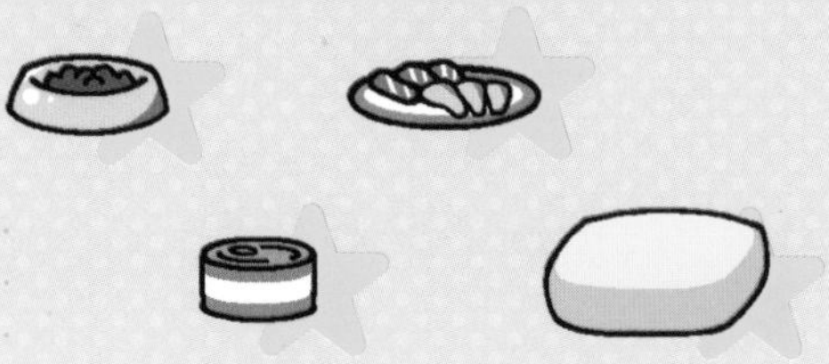

♥ memo

Neko Atsume Haiku
Kitty Collector
SEASONS OF THE KITTY

Original Concept by Hit-Point
VIZ MEDIA EDITION

NEKOATSUME OFFICIAL BOOK NEKOATSUME BIYORI
©2017 Hit-Point
All Rights Reserved.
First published in Japan in 2015 by KADOKAWA CORPORATION ENTERBRAIN
English translation rights arranged with KADOKAWA CORPORATION ENTERBRAIN

English Adaptation 🐾 **Annette Roman**
Translation 🐾 **Tetsuichiro Miyaki**
Original Design 🐾 **Maiko Ichinoseki**
Design 🐾 **Alice Lewis**
Editor 🐾 **Annette Roman**

🐾 **WRITING STAFF:**
Yumiko Dezawa: 25, 30, 31, 45, 46, 56, 58, 63, 72, 83, 90, 92, 94, 108, 109, 118, 124, 125
Yukiko Uno: 14, 15, 54, 62, 74, 78, 86, 106, 113, 115, 120, 121
Shiinaromi: 17, 22, 28, 33, 44, 47, 53, 82, 84, 114
Azusa Kumagai: 34
Shinichi Okamoto: 12, 16, 18, 20, 21, 24, 26, 32, 42, 48, 50, 52, 57, 60, 61, 64, 75, 76, 79, 80, 85, 88, 91, 93, 102, 103, 104, 110, 112, 116, 122

🐾 **ILLUSTRATIONS:**
Sekiyayaya
Sarukoro Mizutani
Kino Takahashi
Maiko Ichinoseki

Printed in China

Published by VIZ Media, LLC
P.O. Box 77010
San Francisco, CA 94107

10 9 8 7 6 5 4 3 2 1
First printing, February 2018

viz.com